Correctional Manipulation

By Anthony Gangi

About the Author...

For over thirteen years, Anthony Gangi has worked in the correctional setting dealing with both male and female offenders. He served on the custody level and has moved through the ranks from line officer to supervisor. With a background in Psychology, he has become a leading expert in inmate manipulation and, during his time as an instructor, he has had the chance to meet, on a national level, with other professionals in his field. Anthony Gangi is currently a columnist for correctionsone.com and an active writer for corrections.com. He is currently the host of Tier Talk which can be found at www.spreaker.com.Tier Talk is the only show on the air for corrections, by corrections, about corrections.

We Are Connected To Our Environment And The Situations That Occur!

Situations are extremely powerful. While some people choose to focus on internal motivations, you must never overlook the power of external constraints, or pressures. Now, situations can sometimes be invisible. Which means that those from the outside may not understand the true pressures, or constraints that those, on the inside, face? Let's explore this a little bit, shall we. Frontline employees know their jobs, but, often times, they have to deal with changes that are driven by those who only have an outside perspective. More concern is directed at incentive and/or budget, as opposed to the subtle environmental changes that can drastically affect those who are immediate to that situation of change.

These detrimental changes can only be brought to mind by those who have experience on the front line. There are those who are subordinate to the system and faithfully follow these new policies and procedure that will end up being the scapegoat when it becomes discovered, through error, or misuse, that safety and security was sacrificed. Recently, news had centered on an area known as the "Honor Block." It is an area within a maximum security prison that allows for certain inmates, in contrary to their status, to live in an environment with minimal restrictions. These inmates have to meet a certain criteria based on good behavior and institutional adjustment.

Just as a reminder, some of the inmates, who were approved for the "Honor Block," still have major sentences to complete.

This "Honor Block" was brought to life in the hope that inmates will see a positive side to good behavior and, therefore, it becomes an incentive. Those that would argue that the "Honor Block" provides incentive should realize that true incentive can only come from within. External motivation should not be the only incentive that we look towards to promote good behavior. We need to encourage change that begins from within. Now, I want to investigate this a little further. First, let's define honor. Honor is defined by Merriam Webster as respect that is given to someone who is admired, good reputation, good quality or character as judged by other people. It is within this definition we have a conflict. By choosing the name "Honor Block," are we instilling all the above mentioned qualities and values that define the word honor into the inmates that reside within that block. In essence, by using that term to define that cell block, are we saying, "these inmates can be trusted." Now, for the most part, inmates that have a lot of time have a different perspective than those who are on their way out. The latter is looking to better themselves and prepare for the outside world, while the former are looking for ways to circumvent the system and maintain their sense of self-control. When we begin to invest in programs that are brought to light from those on the outside, we need to look at the possible consequences, both good and bad.

In this case, the "Honor Block" instills a sense of trust that can easily define the environment and create a situation that can easily lead to undue familiarity. By no way am I excusing the behavior of those who are directly involved in aiding and abetting an escape, but, in order to learn, we must look at all the elements involved. Corrections is a job that is defined by routine. The work is rather monotonous and can easily lead to complacency. As the days progress, complacency can easily become the norm. Inmates that look to control the system, that still have major time to do, will look to exploit this vulnerability. They will do whatever is necessary so they can gain a sense of control. When the environment itself shows a sense of trust, then we have created a monster.

If we want to look at how manipulation can occur, we need to look at the target and the situation that was presented. If the target becomes vulnerable, they may find themselves looking to the environment for help. If the environment is defined by trust then this person is in trouble. I say this because it is human nature to look to the environment to define the situation we are in. When we are filled with ambiguity, we look to others. It is at this point that we are most vulnerable. If the inmates reside within an environment that seems to be built on trust, are we not creating the perfect situation for a manipulative inmate to exploit? This type of environment brings about situations that will lead to inconsistency and unfairness. That is why, when programs are created, we need to look first at security issues. This is when it becomes necessary to talk to the frontline because they know best.

Corrections is an environment that is unique. It centers on a culture that few will ever be able to understand. Working with individuals for years, we have to remember they are felons first. That is the thought that must remain paramount through our career. But, on another note, the manipulative inmate wants to make you forget that they are felons. They try to connect with you on a personal level that will help them to achieve their end game. Remember, if we get emotionally involved, we become compromised. When an inmate begins their game, it is subtle and slow moving. It is not something that is immediately recognized and the changes that occur to the targeted staff member are slow. When the targeted staff member begins to feel that something is not right, they may begin to look to their environment for a sense of confirmation, as to whom they are and the role they must play. If that environment fails to remind them of their prescribed role, the inmate can easily move forward.

Again, ideas that come from the outside need to take into account the human element. This would relate to the automatic processes that can easily be exploited by a manipulative inmate. In this case, we need to look outside of the targeted individuals. We need to ask ourselves about the environment and the situation that was created based on an incentive program. All in all, if certain words are used every day, like "honor and trustee", what are we telling the staff member? Let's face it, games will be played and some will fall and others will rise, but the last thing we ever want to do, is create the situation in which a manipulative inmate can thrive. Therefore, go to the frontline and ask them, "What are the pros and cons of implementing such a program." You figured, if they are going to get blamed, may as well give them a fighting chance.

Introduction

Writing a book on inmate manipulation can be a very trying effort. Multiple tactics can be employed by the manipulative inmate that center on covert methods that include minimal compliance, or misdirection. These methods are covertly pushed forward by the inmate in an effort to gain ground and go on the offensive. As an instructor on inmate manipulation, I have to maintain a curriculum that adapts to the changing methods employed by the inmate, as well as prepare the defenses needed so staff can save ground and, if needed, move forward.

Manipulation by an inmate is an all out effort to gain ground. Gaining ground gives the inmate the control needed to regulate their stay within the confines of their respective institutions. It is at this point, I must highlight, that staff CAN NEVER GIVE GROUND. Whether, by the inmate's use of covert aggression, or overt force, a staff must hold their ground and, at all times, maintain and enforce their sense of control. For a manipulator, losing ground is not an option and, therefore, if the inmate senses that you will not maneuver your position they will move onto an easier target. Inmates maneuver their manipulative tactic in a manner that maintains minimal effort and greatest reward. By this standard, a staff member, for example, who feels the constant "need to please" becomes an easy target to exploit. The staff member's "need to please" becomes the vulnerability needed for the inmate to gain ground. The inmate will view this staff member as being weak and, therefore, easily vulnerable to manipulation.

As mentioned in this book, there are multiple manipulative tactics that can be employed by the inmate population that directly relate to either the vulnerability of the staff member, or certain situational factors that can be used by the inmate to gain ground. These tactics that are employed by the inmate fit perfectly within the context of the situation and create, in a sense, a collective effort between the staff and the inmate. I say the word collective because manipulation is a two way street and, therefore, a manipulative inmate cannot gain ground unless the staff member gives in. The inmate will seize the opportunity and plan their attack in manner that fits the situation at hand. If you are soft, the inmates will walk all over you. If you are strictly by the book, the inmates will learn your routine. If you can be made to feel obligated, the inmates will begin doing "favors for you". If you are down on your luck, an inmate will know exactly what to say to lift your spirits. If you have an inability to be consistent, an inmate will persist until your "no" becomes a "yes". If you become personal with an inmate, the inmate will use your personal information and create a bond that stretches outside of professionalism and into the world of undue familiarity. These are just a list of some of the tactics the inmate population has perfected over time. It is within the staff member to discover their own sense of vulnerability and change it into strength.

This book is centered on two factors: who we are and who we must be. At times, this can bring conflict because there are certain qualities that define the essence of our being. Having said that, who we are and who we must be provides the separation needed between our work and home. Maintaining that balance provides the staff member with the tools needed to defend their position against manipulative inmates and, if need be, push forward.

Inmates have all the time needed to employ what tactic fits best. The inmate's world is centered on their ability to observe staff. The staff members that are considered weak will be separated from other staff members by methods that bring about the "us vs. them" mentality. The inmates separate the weak staff members from support staff because they know that through our unified brotherhood/sisterhood we cannot be broken. In their mind, the further the inmate can separate staff, the more likely their end game will result in a major reward. *On a side note, even if there is no reward in sight, inmates have so much time to kill that they may simply find enjoyment in just the game being played.*

Communication is key. This book is a must read for all levels of correctional staff, from custody to civilian. We need to build a bond, so collectively; we can become a unified, unstoppable, force. Somewhere along the line we have lost that connection between civilian and custody and, therefore, we need to bring that connection back. Collectively, custody and civilian staff form a bond that nothing, but omnipotence should be able to break.

In closing, corrections is a profession that has more DOWNS than it does UPS. Our public service is never seen in full light and recognition for a job well done rarely ever comes. In essence, this is a good thing because the brothers and sisters that have committed themselves to this field do the job for one sole purpose; WE ARE OUR BROTHER'S AND OUR SISTER'S KEEPER. It is behind the wall that we realize that we are our brother's and our sister's keeper. If you see an officer or staff member in trouble, talk to them. Show them support. At the end of the day, the manipulative tactics that are being employed may be so minimal (at first) that the staff member may not realize they are being "PLAYED". This book can help you gain the ground needed so control can go back into the hands of the "KEEPER". BY READING THIS BOOK, YOU MAY BE THE ONE PROVIDING THE ADVICE TO SOMEONE IN NEED. THIS

SOMEONE MAY NOT ONLY BE A THREAT TO THEMSELVES, BUT CAN EVEN BE A MORE SERIOUS THREAT TO OTHERS.

THIS BOOK IS NOT AN EXCUSE MEANT TO ALLEVIATE THE BLAME, RATHER IT WAS WRITTEN JUST AS AN INFORMATIVE GUIDE TO HELP EXPLAIN WHY PEOPLE DO WHAT THEY DO. BY KNOWING THE INFORMATION THAT FOLLOWS, WE CAN GET A BETTER UNDERSTANDING OF THE ACTIONS THAT ARE NEEDED TO PREVENT.

Chapter 1 (What is Social Psychology?)

We cannot be distinguished from our situations, for they form us and decide our possibilities"

Jean Paul Sartre (1946)

The statement written above goes against what most people tend to believe. Most people would have you believe that the way an individual acts, in any given situation, can easily be determined by the individual's disposition. Therefore, many laypersons make judgments, or predications, based on the internal qualities of the individual (disposition) that can be seen as rather stable through time. This is known as the **fundamental attribution error**. Social Psychologists would be quick to remind those people that the situation an individual encounters are very powerful and should never be overlooked.

Social Psychologists conduct studies in a wide array of areas that can easily be applied to our everyday life. There are three central themes of great concern that have defined the field of Social Psychology and have become the cornerstone of development for all those directly related to the field. These three central themes have managed to cut across most of the research topics in the field of Social Psychology. Starting with the earliest and most obvious, Social Psychologists began with the power of the group as a normative influence, then they moved on to the centrality of subjective meaning and interpretation and, finally, an emphasis on the "non obvious" experimental demonstration. Let's take a second to discuss the first two themes, being that they are the most pertinent to the reading provided. By discussing these two themes a bit, I hope to provide you with a better understanding of the work that is done by those in the field of Social Psychology.

Social Influences (Group Influences)

A group can be defined as a unit composed of two or more people who interact and depend on each other in some way. Now, even though this is a rather simple definition, it fits quite well with the purpose of this book. The features of a group consist of the norms that determine the appropriate behavior, the roles that are assigned to people that determine what behaviors and responsibilities people should take on, a communication structure that determines who talks to whom within the group and a power structure that determines how much authority and influence group members have.

Example

In the world of corrections, our working environment consists of policies and procedures **(norms)** *that define our prescribed roles. These policies and procedures determine the appropriate behavior within the job function we are trusted to perform. Each correctional facility has multiple departments which must work in unison so the overall goal of the agency can be fulfilled. Each department has employees who have a* **role** *to play. Each role is fundamental to the success of the agency as a whole.* **Communication** *is a key element in corrections and there is a structure that must be maintained for the safety and security of the agency. Finally, corrections is considered a paramilitary unit and, within that above mentioned word, corrections must maintain a* **power structure** *that determines how much authority and influence each group member has (ranks, management, etc.).*

This is just an example, and, what is mentioned above can be sub-divided by department and even further by cliques within that department, but the main idea behind what is written above is to just simply show that our working environment is defined by the multiple features that relate to groups and their activities. Of course, we still have the inmate population which will be discussed later in the book.

Moving forward, as we discuss social influences (group influences) and how it directly relates to the field of corrections, we will go into studies that have proven to be quite applicable to our working environment. One such study is Solomon Asch's Conformity Study. Solomon Asch discovered that there are multiple factors that can influence conformity. These factors include the size of the group, the unanimity of the group, the insecurity of the individual in the group and the admiration the individual holds for the group . He also discovered the many reasons why an individual conforms. These reasons include the individual's need to feel accepted by the group (normative influence), the individual's fear of rejection by the group, the information that is provided to the individual by the group (informational social influence), and the need, or want, for material and social reward.

Other group dynamics at play relate to **group polarization** (the dominant point of view of the group often tends to be strengthened to a more extreme position after a group discussion), **group cohesiveness** (the strength of the liking and commitment group members have towards each other and to the group), **minority influence** (a committed minority viewpoint can change the majority opinion in the group), **deindividuation** (when people are part of a large group they may feel aroused and anonymous), **groupthink** (the tendency for a close knit group to emphasize consensus at the expense of critical thinking and rational decision-making), and **social facilitation** (in some cases, individuals may perform better, or worse when others are present). All the above mentioned terms are relevant in the world of corrections and they are at play every second of every day. Chapter 2 will discuss group cohesiveness and conflict and how they can easily be employed in an effort to manipulate and gain a sense of control. Chapter 3 will discuss conformity and why individuals commit to behaviors that go against their beliefs.

Subjectivity

This may come as a bit of a surprise, but no two people see the world in exactly the same way. Each person percieves, comprehends, and interprets the world around them in a manner that reflects their own personal biases, feelings and experiences. This is known as *Subjective Construal*. In essence, we don't objectively take reality in and see it at face value; rather we subjectively take reality in and reflect, or construct, the world around us.

For example, if an individual is having a bad day, then their mood will have an effect on how they see the world and interpret the behaviors of others. So, Charlie is having a bad day at the office and appears to be angry at the world. While leaving his office, a fellow employee bumps into him. The employee apologizes for the accidental bump, but Charlie believes that the employee bumped into him on purpose. His fellow employee tries to convince him that it was an accident, but Charlie is not hearing it. In Charlie's world, his negative affect has primed him to think the world is against him. The accidental bump from his fellow employee becomes a push. On the flipside, if Charlie had a great day at the office, his mood would interpret the bump as just a bump, and, therefore, would be quick to laugh it off.

We need to always keep in mind that no two people see the exact same thing. And when we go back to evaluate the situation, we must never close our eyes to the perspective of the individual going through the situation. We need to try our best to see things from their perspective and remain objective. This is not an easy task, but, in order for us to learn, we need to remove all judgement and approach the situation in a manner that is objective and free from bias.

On another note, for those who decide to Monday night quarterback and make a judgement on a situation that has already been resolved, your knowledge of the total situation, including the outcome, will immediately separate you from those who went through it. To them, the situation was novel and they have to construct their world on the fly with no prior knowledge of any outcome. For those that Monday night quarterback, you have the entire picture at play, including the outcome, and your construction will be more informative and detailed. Therefore, you will never be able to see the situation as they did, because, for you, the situation is entirely different. Please keep that in mind when you are put into a position where judgement of one's actions falls on you. Take into account the power of the situation at hand and how one's perception of the situation may be limited to the amount of information they are given at the time. Again, this is not easy, but, in order to understand the choices an individual makes, you have to go outside the disposition of the individual and see what situational factors had control of their immediate behavior.

Corrections is Law Enforcement

In closing this chapter, I just want to put a reminder out there for anyone who questions the work of those behind the wall. Below is an article I wrote for correction.com that highlights Correctional Officers as law enforcement professionals and a true credit behind the safety and security of the public.

A riot has broken out in the mess hall and within seconds two suited teams stand at the ready. In a military fashion the team members enter the mess hall and form a line between order and chaos. Before marching forward, they wonder if today will be that tragic day. They clash. Inmates fight to gain ground, but the suited teams armed with batons maintain control. Lives are saved as inmates who are not involved are quickly escorted to safety. Those who chose to riot are subdued and escorted to medical for evaluations. Today, the line could not be broken.

For the moment the riot has been quelled. The suited teams hang up their gear and movement within the prison goes back to normal. Today they were lucky. Tomorrow, who knows?

Within these walls, and defined by many as turn keys, jail guards, or overpaid babysitters, are men and women who live and die by their sworn oath to protect and serve, men and women who have earned their badges and belong to the brotherhood/sisterhood of law enforcement professionals. They are correctional officers. They stand tall in the face of adversity and risk their lives to maintain an environment that is conducive to rehabilitation. It's an environment that promises hope to the hopeless.

But, who cares? As attention gets driven to the outside, and those who work the streets become the standard definition of a law enforcement professional, they, who stand alone on the inside, simply get overlooked.

Recent cries of civil unrest on the streets have become the center of attention as small portions of the citizenry take an aggressive stance against their protectors. This may feel a little strange to those on the outside, but to correctional officers, this defines their existence. An existence that is centered on a society who wishes to violently break away from authority and find utopia amongst the subsequent chaos and disorder that would presume. Law and order is all that they have to maintain control over a society dominated by hatred and greed.

There are some who will read this article and quickly belittle what correctional officers do from a perspective that is far removed from the dangers that lie within. Their limited knowledge of who correctional officers are will cast doubt in the hearts of others who believe and have faith in the services they provide. By remaining on the outside, those with a negative view will always be limited. But, if they could experience the correctional officers world, unrestricted from the dangers that wait, they would see and feel firsthand that corrections have evolved. It's a noble and honest law enforcement profession.

Jails and prisons are no longer considered warehouses with little personal interactions limited to a simple turn of a key. Rehabilitation has now become the main focus and interpersonal staff interactions with the criminal element are made every day.

Correctional officers level of control relates to their ability to enforce the rules and regulations that govern a community in constant movement. They are the 'keepers' who remain surrounded by the 'enemy.' They remain weaponless as they walk the tiers. Their ability to communicate becomes paramount.

Correctional officers need to remain firm, fair and consistent in their dealings with the inmate population. They need to show no fear in a world that is dominated by predators and aggressors. They are the law within these walls and anything less than direct obedience from the inmate population is seen as a threat to their existence.

Their interactions with the offender consist of multiple elements that define the role of law enforcement professional; minus the recognition. These professionals stop assaults, prevent suicides and homicides, suppress gang activity, seize contraband (weapons, drugs, etc.), conduct investigations, make arrests, and most importantly, prevent escapes. All of these elements can be furthered used to assist other law enforcement agencies in maintaining a safe and secure society. It's by this definition they have secured their place in the law enforcement family.

But there may still be some who deny corrections is law enforcement. They maintain a perspective in which corrections and law enforcement remain unequal and any chance to create a sense of equality gets push aside. As law enforcement across the country is under attack, this kind of mockery is misplaced.

Therefore in the eyes of those who oppose, correctional officers become a reflection of the criminal element they supervise. This reflection presents a major conflict because it separates them from their brothers/sisters in blue and brings them closer to the offenders in their charge. The more they stand in isolation, the more they begin to question their importance. It is within that last statement that some may mistakenly see being a police officer as a step up from working in the 'tombs.'

As law enforcement professionals, correctional officers run parallel with police officers and their contribution to society is embedded in the personal sacrifices that they make on a daily basis to maintain their sense of control over the 'kept' and ensure that those who are locked away, are given the chance to become productive members of society.

Even though correctional officers may stand unrecognized by those who remain outside, they are still motivated to do their job by their sworn duty to protect and serve. Being a professional means you do the job because the job has to get done. Correctional officers make sacrifices the public may never know, nor may never care. They risk their lives everyday in *service to the public. In their fight, they have lost many, but continue to remain strong. Failure to recognize their importance is a failure to recognize a brother or sister who would die for the same things those on the outside represent. Embrace the complete circle of law enforcement and acknowledge those who lurk in the shadows and perform their services in the dark. Embrace them as law enforcement professionals and see them as they see you: one united blue family.*

Chapter 2: Our Need to Belong/Conflict and Cohesiveness

Since there have only been very little social experiments done with corrections in mind, we have to look outside the box and become inventive with the results. In short, we have to combine the results of what has been used in the real world and modify those results a bit to fit into our world; the world of corrections. In an effort to be brief and concise, I will only bring to light the theories that have elements that can relate to our field. This relationship will be drawn from real life scenarios that exist behind the prison wall. Keep in mind, the experiments that will be discussed have been replicated and the results have been validated.

Each chapter will begin with one scenario that has been constructed by those who work in our field. The scenarios in this book are based on reality and will be used as a reference when we apply the results of the experiments, or theories that will subsequently be mentioned. For example, this chapter will have one scenario of reference that can be used to help connect the experiments, or theories, of the past with our present working environment.

Scenario 1:

Correctional Officer Recruit John Smith is fifteen minutes away from finishing his first shift on the job. It was an uneventful night and, in just a few minutes, it will be time for him to hand over the keys to the next shift. Looking at his watch, he realizes that he has enough time for one more tour. He closes his logbook, secures it in his desk, and begins to walk around. One wing is rather quiet with most inmates on their beds watching tv. As he begins to walk down two wing, he hears, what seems to be, an argument between two inmates. Correctional Officer Recruit John Smith quickly addresses the issue and manages to get both of the inmates to calm down. He exits the wing, and, just before he heads down three wing, he begins to wonder if both of those inmates should have been separated. He doesn't think the argument was that bad, but there is always the chance, that when he leaves, the argument may progress to something further. At this moment, with five minutes left before his shift ends, Correctional Officer Recruit John Smith picks up the phone and requests for his area supervisor to come to his unit.

The area supervisor enters the unit and quickly motions to the time as he begins to yell at the Correctional Officer Recruit. The supervisor, being more concerned with going home then with the issue at hand, becomes loud and irate. At this point, all the inmates, who reside in the unit, can hear the supervisor rant and rave. As the next shift officer is seen at the door ready to enter, the supervisor motions for them to wait outside while he continues to belittle the Correctional Officer Recruit. The Correctional Officer Recruit, embarrassed, puts his head down in utter defeat. The supervisor exits the unit and motions for the next shift officer to come in and take control of the unit. At this point, the Correctional Officer Recruit hands over the keys and slowly leaves the unit.

The next day, the Correctional Officer Recruit is placed in the same unit. An inmate approaches him. THE GAME IS ON!

<u>Maslow's Hierarchy of Needs</u>

The above mentioned inmate is about to employ a subtle tactic known as **"Us vs. Them."** This is a tactic that totally exploits the power of our internal need to belong. It deals first with group conflict and then group cohesiveness. Before we go into this process, let's first take a look at **Abraham Maslow's hierarchy of needs.**

In 1943, Abraham Maslow wrote a paper titled, "A Theory of Human Motivation." He stated that human motivation moves through a pattern that begins with the **physiological needs** of the individual and works its way up to **self actualization.** Eventually, Maslow's theory would be fully expressed in his 1954 book **Motivation and Personality,** which is still used today as a framework for sociology, management training and secondary and higher psychology instruction.

Maslow's hierarchy of needs is often represented as a pyramid where the fundamental, or most basic needs (deficiency needs) are seen in the first three levels of the pyramid and the secondary, or higher level, needs are closer to the top. Maslow believed that the fundamental, or most basic needs must be successfully met first before the individual will strongly desire the secondary, or higher level, needs. At the very bottom of the pyramid Maslow placed **Physiological needs**. Basically, these are the physical needs necessary for our survival (air, water, food, etc.). Once these needs are successfully met, an individual can then move forward to **Safety needs**. Safety needs refer to personal security, financial security, health and well being, and a safety net against accidents/illnesses and their adverse impacts. Again, once the needs of the second level is successfully met, movement to the third becomes plausible. At the third level of the pyramid, Maslow placed **Love and Belonging**. At this level, Maslow believed that all individuals have the want, or need, to be loved and to belong (family, friends, intimacy, etc.). Maslow also believed that humans have the need to feel accepted amongst their social groups. This is the need that will be paramount in our discussion of the scenario mentioned above. Moving forward, once this level has been successfully met, travel now begins to take us to the fourth level; the secondary, or higher level, needs. **Esteem** becomes our next stop on the Maslow hierarchy's pyramid. At this level, Maslow expressed that all humans have a need to feel respected and to be accepted and valued by others. And, finally, we have **Self-actualization**. Self-actualization can only be reached after all prior levels have successfully been met. Self-actualization basically refers to a person's full potential. In essence, Maslow believed that if an individual is to achieve this level, they must have the desire to accomplish everything that they can do, so they can become the most they can be.

In a nutshell, that is a brief description of Maslow's hierarchy of needs. As stated earlier for the aforementioned scenario, I want to focus on level three; love and belonging. It is at this level of the pyramid that an individual becomes most vulnerable to the "Us vs. Them" tactic. With that in mind, let's take another look at scenario one.

Scenario 1:

Correctional Officer Recruit John Smith is fifteen minutes away from finishing his first shift on the job. It was an uneventful night and, in just a few minutes, it will be time for him to hand over the keys to the next shift. Looking at his watch, he realizes that he has enough time for one more tour. He closes his logbook, secures it in his desk, and begins to walk around. One wing is rather quiet with most inmates on their beds watching tv. As he begins to walk down two wing, he hears, what seems to be, an argument between two inmates. Correctional Officer Recruit John Smith quickly addresses the issue and manages to get both of the inmates to calm down. He exits the wing, and, just before he heads down three wing, he begins to wonder if both of those inmates should have been separated. He doesn't think the argument was that bad, but there is always the chance, that when he leaves, the argument may progress to something further. At this moment, with five minutes left before his shift ends, Correctional Officer Recruit John Smith picks up the phone and requests for his area supervisor to come to his unit.

The area supervisor enters the unit and quickly motions to the time as he begins to yell at the Correctional Officer Recruit. The supervisor, being more concerned with going home then with the issue at hand, becomes loud and irate. At this point, all the inmates, who reside in the unit, can hear the supervisor rant and rave. As the next shift officer is seen at the door ready to enter, the supervisor motions for them to wait outside while he continues to belittle the Correctional Officer Recruit. The Correctional Officer Recruit, embarrassed, puts his head down in utter defeat. The supervisor exits the unit and motions for the next shift officer to come in and take control of the unit. At this point, the Correctional Officer Recruit hands over the keys and slowly leaves the unit.

The next day, the Correctional Officer Recruit is placed in the same unit. An inmate approaches him. THE GAME IS ON!

Breakdown of Scenario 1

Through the supervisor's actions, a situation has been created and can easily be exploited by the inmate population. A situation that will build from the inmate's ability to become immediately empathetic, partnered with the staff member's need to save face. The staff member has become vulnerable. This vulnerability stems from a created situation by the supervisor in which the manipulative inmate is now able to exploit.

Let's first analyze this scenario by looking at Correctional Officer Recruit John Smith and his situation. Let's try to get an understanding of how he sees his situation (subjective construal). Let's see how he perceives, comprehends, and interprets his world and, most importantly, the behavior and actions of others.

In understanding manipulation and how it presents itself, either covert or overt, an individual must understand the power of the situation. For the staff member, in the above mentioned scenario, their situation has changed and is now being controlled by emotion. As for the inmates, the situation presented to them now shows a staff member who thoughts lie outside of logic and, instead, stem from emotional blindness.

For the Recruit, he may feel a natural reaction to redeem himself by venting to the empathetic ear displayed by the "overly concerned" inmate. At this point, the inmate's advice may be centered in a way to employ the tactic that was mentioned above, "Us vs. them".

In order to move forward with this tactic, the inmate will expose many techniques that highlight concern, friendliness, and similarity. These techniques are used to disguise the inmate's true intention. The true intention, mentioned above, is centered on changing the Recruit's perception of the aforementioned inmate. Eventually, the change in perception creates a different situation for the Recruit. This Recruit may no longer see an inmate as an inmate. The empathetic ear displayed by the inmate has led this Recruit to believe that the inmate understands their situation and, therefore, is now being led down a manipulative path that was created by the supervisor's unprofessionalism an aided by the inmate population.

The Recruit's need to feel competent lies on their need to justify their situation. Having demeaned the Recruit in view of the inmate population, the supervisor has created a situation in which this above mentioned Recruit may feel the need to redeem himself. This redemption may come in the hands of an empathetic ear provided by the "overly concerned" inmate.

Moving forward, we must remember, we also have group dynamics at play. So, let's go back to the beginning again so we can get a full understanding of the group dynamics at play.

Now, Correctional Officer Recruit John Smith is fresh out the academy. During his time in the academy, the recruits were put through exercises that promote group solidarity. The instructors do what they can to solidify the trainees, so, when they enter the facility, there is a strong brotherhood/sisterhood that forms. This is meant to remind the trainee of the group they belong to. Once the trainee becomes a Recruit and leaves the academy, the real world begins. Inside the academy, the trainee is isolated from any forces that look to destroy the group. Through isolation, the group become very tight and very well knit. But, once they enter the real world, the Correctional Officer Recruit is no longer isolated from the forces that look to break that bond. Therefore, the moment the Correctional Officer Recruit enters the real world, their group solidarity will be tested, as well as their convictions.

As mentioned above, the opportune situation was created by the supervisor for the inmates to exploit. The inmates witnessed, firsthand, the Correctional Officer Recruit get belittled and now it's their chance to build the recruit back up. For the recruit, being belittled made him feel incompetent and separated from those who are suppose to be his brothers/sisters. Now, not only is the Correctional Officer Recruit looking to redeem himself, he is also looking to find someone he can relate to that will see things from his perspective. It is through that perspective, a similarity will be drawn that will be used to connect Correctional Recruit John Smith with the inmate population.

From the inmate's perspective, he knows that the Correctional Officer Recruit is vulnerable. His objective at this point is to further divide this Correctional Officer Recruit from the rest of staff. When the conversation begins between the manipulative inmate and the Recruit, the inmate will pretend to be sympathetic to the Correctional Officer Recruit's needs. He will tell the Recruit that the supervisor was wrong in treating him that way. That no one deserves to be treated that way, especially if they were only doing their job. He will also be quick to mention that the other inmates on the wing also feel the supervisor was in the wrong. The Correctional Officer Recruit will quickly agree, because if the inmates are wrong then the Recruit would be admitting that he deserved to be belittled.

Now, once the Recruit agrees, separation begins to occur. In order for this game to work and the "Us vs. Them" tactic to be a success, the inmate needs the Recruit to separate himself from staff and then for the recruit to find his sense of belonging amongst the inmate population. As mentioned above, the inmate does this by building conflict between the other staff members and the Recruit. Once they build that conflict, they begin to isolate the Recruit from the other staff members. The inmate may do this by simply forming a bond between him and the Recruit that is easily seen by other staff members. Eventually, the other staff members will see this and will slowly move themselves away from the Recruit and begin treating him like an outcast. (Staff become the out-group for the Recruit and the in-group is now moving towards the inmate population.) Once the Recruit is out casted, the inmate will begin a strong effort to bring the Recruit into his group (the inmate population). They welcome the Recruit in and strengthen his connection by continuing to instill conflict between the Recruit and the rest of staff. The greater the conflict, the more attached the Recruit becomes to the inmate population. Once this connection get solidified, and the Recruit has been turned away from his peers, the inmates become the Recruit's only connection; his only source for information. In essence, they feign sympathy for the belittled staff member, bring him over to their group, create greater conflict with the Recruit and staff, and, finally, use that conflict to get the Recruit to become more solidified with those that now accept him (inmate population).

Situational Concerns

As a reminder, in some cases, manipulation can arise through situations that we, as staff members, produce. We need to be logical and prepare ourselves for the consequences, both good and bad, that follow our actions. We need to be objective in our line our work and not be blinded by subjective emotion. Inmates are masters at exploiting chance opportunities and will easily maneuver into position when the opportunity or situation arises. As mentioned above, the "us vs. them" technique is easily employed when a situation arises in which most of the hard work is already done. Staff that has been belittled in public view now becomes an open door to that above mentioned tactic. Overall, we must know that an inmate can take their time and choose who they believe will be the perfect target for manipulation, or we can save them the work by creating a situation in which the target is provided.

Below, is an article that that I wrote and was subsequently published by corrections.com. I believe this article explains the essence of the "Us Vs. Them" Tactic.

"Us vs. Them"

"Us vs. Them" can simply mean, "Divide and conquer." It is at this point we must decide to stand united. Inmates know that if staff remain united, we cannot be conquered. It is in staff's ability to stand tall and trust each other that the unbreakable bond of strength is created. An inmate spends all day looking for a weakness. An inmate needs to find a way to SEPERATE this unbreakable bond that has been created by staff and exploit its vulnerabilities. Inmates know that, individually, we are vulnerable. An inmate knows that manipulative tactics can be better employed by separating staff and then enforcing inmate support. This, in essence, is the beginning of the "Us vs. Them" tactic.

As individuals, we may feel the need, or motivation, to belong or connect. It is within this basic human need that an inmate can easily find a way to divide and conquer staff. The inmate will take advantage of any situation in which staff is perceived as separate from the whole. This separation can occur through the disposition of the staff member, or through a situation that arises in which a staff member has been pushed away from support staff. This separation is paramount and aids the inmate tremendously as they begin to employ their manipulative tactics.

The question now arises; how can staff be separated? It is within these answers that a shield and sword can be created that enables staff to defend their position and then push forward and gain ground. I say gain ground because the inmate's main goal is to gain control and be on the offensive. Inmates employ manipulative tactics in an effort to gain ground and push forward. In order for this to occur, staff members have to be pushed into a defensive position in which the next step committed by the inmate causes the staff member to fall back and lose ground. In essence, a mind game pursues. Inmates have all the time to think their strategy through and plan an offensive that can be easily compared to a game a chess in which the opposing player is thinking 3-5 steps ahead of their opponent.

In relationship to chess, inmates have the time to think things through and every act on their part brings about a reaction from staff that runs in accordance with their well thought out plan. By these standards, if staff remain defensive, staff will never gain ground and will be constantly pushed back by the offensive strategies employed by the manipulative inmate. Inmates will exploit any conflict between staff, or any working conditions that may cause rise to negative effect. Inmates will become that sympathetic ear when that staff member begins to voice their complaints. By listening to staff, the inmate is able to construct a rapport that paints a picture of companionship and trust. By this standard, the inmates are bringing about a group mentality which gives birth to two opposing forces that will formulate into the "US (inmate along with single staff member) vs. Them (the rest of staff)". This is the element that we need to explore.

The intragroup dynamic of any group can be strengthened by the conflict that centers on the outside group, or the intergroup relationship. In short, through the feelings of competition with an outside group, the inner strength of the opposing group is strengthen. The inmate is aware that they must first separate the staff member from the rest of staff and then move them over to the opposing group (inmates). At this point, the inmates can exploit multiple tactics that can relate to sympathy, friendliness, or even similarities (ethnicity, religion). The premise at this point is to get the staff member to drop their guard.

Support staff may begin to spot a change in the, soon to be, separated staff member and may try multiple attempts to warn them that they are being played. These multiple attempts will fail because the staff member will become defensive as they are pulled further and further away from support. On a side note, there are certain signs that support staff can look for so they can recognize a targeted staff member. These signs can include a level of comfortability between staff member and inmate (observed by verbal and non-verbal communication), their inability to communicate with staff, the lack of control in the staff member's respected area, their defense of the inmate population, and, when not assigned to that certain area, the tainted staff member will find themselves there amongst the population.

Moving forward, once the connection between inmates and staff member has been made, it will be reinforced by partnership words (Us) and separation words (Them). Once the staff member has been drawn into the inmate's group, inmates will strengthen the connection by the constant promotion of conflict between staff and the constant promotion of understanding by the inmates. Eventually, the inmates will be able to say freely to the tainted staff member that you are one of us and the staff member will sit in agreement.

The separation that has occurred, powered by inmate maneuverability, gives the tainted staff member the needed justification to switch sides and commit their indiscretions. This tactic can be developed over time, or can be gift wrapped in the form of public conflict that lay in view of the inmate population. Negative verbal expressions about the workplace can also bring about a connection between staff and inmate that can be exploited into a "Us vs. Them". In closing, we, as staff, are only as strong as our weakest link. If we sense that the link is about to be broken, we need to stand behind it and reinforce its strength. One weak link can open us up and make us all vulnerable.

Chapter 3 (Conformity)

For this chapter, I want to break away from the inmate population and talk about peer pressure and conformity. Conformity is defined as a change in the way an individual thinks. I think conformity plays a major role in making a "good" officer go "bad." Sometimes a "good" officer is caught in a situation that is hard for them to define and, within seconds, the situation becomes too powerful for them to resist. The social forces at play push and pull the "good" officer and, before they know it, they are now facing charges over an action that goes against everything they believe. Now, we have to ask ourselves, how does this happen? Let's take a look at another scenario.

Scenario 2

Senior Correctional Officer Joseph Hill has been a committed professional to the field of corrections for over 18 years. He has spent his eighteen years in a minimum security institution and his experience with high level incidences has been rather limited.

Today, Senior Correctional Officer Joseph Hill has just been told, that due to cutbacks, he will be transferred to a maximum security facility. Being subordinate to the system, Correctional Officer Joseph Hill takes the reassignment with no argument. He remains optimistic and reminds himself that this is a chance for him to learn something new. He has heard very little about the prison he is being reassigned to. He knows it goes by the name Gladiator School and, rumor has it, the staff handle business. Most of his career, he has been able to communicate effectively with the inmate population and get the job done. Very seldom in his career did Senior Correctional Officer Joseph Hill have to use physical force. If rumors are true about his new assignment, this may be a first for him. But he feels confident in the sense of the brotherhood/sisterhood that makes up the department and puts all his faith in the new family he is about to encounter.

The following week Senior Correctional Officer Joseph Hill starts his new assignment. SO far, his first day on the job was rather uneventful. Senior Correctional Officer Joseph Hill finds his groove and easily blends in with his new family. There is a brotherhood/sisterhood at this prison that has been reinforced by the history of conflict between staff and inmates. (Again, group dynamics are at play here. The more conflict between staff and inmates, the tighter the intragroup dynamic of each opposing group becomes.)

As the shift is about to come to an end, a code is called. With his heart racing, Senior Correctional Officer Joseph Hill runs to the ready room to suit up for the response. His immediate supervisor organizes the team and, within seconds, the team begins to head to the area of disturbance. Upon entering the scene, Senior Correctional Officer Joseph Hill stands in utter shock. For the first time in his career, he sees three officers punching and kicking an inmate who is secured and causing no resistance. In confusion, he goes to look at the officers behind him, but, before he knows it, the support staff has already entered onto the scene and quickly follows suit by continuing to trample the secured inmate. Senior Correctional Officer Joseph Hill is confused. Yet, even though the actions of these officers go against everything Senior Correctional Officer Joseph Hill believes, within minutes he finds himself, amongst the other officers, committing to acts of violence he never believed he was ever capable of doing. What happened to Senior Correctional Officer Joseph Hill? Has he changed, or is there alot here at play that may have caused Joe to react in manner that goes against everything he believes?

Let's Talk About Conformity

The Asch line experiments, which were conducted in the 1950's, dealt directly with conformity and attempted to answer why individuals conform to behaviors that go against their beliefs. Solomon Asch, the individual who conducted the line experiment, stated that "most social acts have to be understood in their setting and lose meaning if isolated. No error in thinking about social facts is more serious than the failure to see their place and function."

He began his study with a primary interest in how group behavior can influence the behavior of the individual. For this study, there was a long table that sat eight individuals (7 were confederates and in on the experiment). Directly in front of them, the experimenter would hold a card with one target line and three comparison lines. For the participants, all they had to do was figure out which comparison line matched the target line. For each card that is shown, the participants answer by going down the line and answering one by one. The person who is being tested is the 8th person and last to answer each trial. On the first two trials, all the participants give the obvious answer and therefore, the participant, who is being tested faces no conflict. But, on the third trial, something unique happens. The experimenter shows a card in which the answer is just as obvious, but this time the six participants give the wrong answer. When it gets to the person being tested, the 8th person, instead of stating the obvious answer, they conform and go with the majority. This happens multiple times through the trials. (On a side note, when the person being tested was alone, with no one else around, they made errors less then 1 % of the time. When they were in groups, 75% of those being tested conformed at least once. And, finally, 37 percent of those being tested gave the wrong answer every time the group did.)

Now, remember, there was no obvious pressure to conform to the group. That is a key element that we need to keep in mind when we break down the scenario mentioned above. When the person being tested was asked, "why did you go against your better judgment," some answered that they feared being ridiculed by the group. This is known as ***normative social influence***. Normative Social Influence refers to an individual who modifies their behavior, so they can better fit in with those around them. Others had answered that they doubted their own responses. If all the other participants were stating a different answer, then that must be the correct one. This is known as ***informational influence***. Informational Influence means that an individual changes their behavior because they feel that the other members of the group are better informed. In essence, they deferred to the group's judgement. For those who didn't conform, they came across as being more confident.

Now, let's take a look again at Scenario 2 and evaluate the situation Senior Correctional Officer Joseph Hill is in.

Scenario 2

Senior Correctional Officer Joseph Hill has been a committed professional to the field of corrections for over 18 years. He has spent his eighteen years in a minimum security institution and his experience with high level incidences has been rather limited.

Today, Senior Correctional Officer Joseph Hill has just been told, that due to cutbacks, he will be transferred to a maximum security facility. Being subordinate to the system, Correctional Officer Joseph Hill takes the reassignment with no argument. He remains optimistic and reminds himself that this is a chance for him to learn something new. He has heard very little about the prison he is being reassigned to. He knows it goes by the name

Gladiator school and, rumor has it, the staff handle business. Most of his career, he has been able to communicate effectively with the inmate population and get the job done. Very seldom in his career did Senior Correctional Officer Joseph Hill have to use physical force. If rumors are true, this may be a first for him. But he feels confident in the sense of the brotherhood/sisterhood that makes up the department and puts all his faith in the new family he is about to encounter.

So far, his first day on the job was rather uneventful. Senior Correctional Officer Joseph Hill finds his groove and easily blends in with his new family. There is a brotherhood/sisterhood at this prison that has been reinforced by the history of conflict between staff and inmates. (Again, group dynamics are at play here. The more conflict between staff and inmates, the tighter the intragroup dynamic of each opposing group becomes.) As the shift is about to come to an end, a code is called. Senior Correctional Officer Joseph Hill, with his heart racing, runs to the ready room to suit up for the response. His immediate supervisor organizes the team and, within seconds, the team begins to head to the area of disturbance. Upon entering the scene, Senior Correctional Officer Joseph Hill stands in utter shock. For the first time in his career, he sees three officers punching and kicking an inmate who is secured and causing no resistance. He goes to say something to the officer behind him, but, before he knows it, the support staff has already entered onto the scene and follow suit by continuing to trample the secured inmate. Senior Correctional Officer Joseph Hill is confused. Yet, even though the actions of these officers go against everything Senior Correctional Officer Joseph Hill believes, within minutes he finds himself, amongst the other officers, committing to acts of violence he never believed he was ever capable of doing. What happened to Senior Correctional Officer Joseph Hill? Has he changed, or is there a lot here at play that may have caused Joe to react in manner that goes against everything he believes?

Breakdown of Scenario 2

Now, we already have an idea of the kind of officer Joseph Hill is. It is time for us to try to understand how Senior Correctional Officer Joseph Hill constructed the situation in his head (**subjective construal**). We must always remember that two people seeing the same exact thing will interpret it differently. Reason being, no individual passively takes in reality without reflective thought. We must remember that each individual has their own experience and biases that will filter the information being presented and, therefore, will aid in their interpretation of the situation. This of course happens without us knowing. So, where does that leave us with Joseph?

First off, the social situation, Senior Correctional Officer Joseph Hill is in, has changed his behavior. He has succumbed, or conformed, to the sometimes covert power of peer pressure. When Senior Correctional Officer Joseph Hill looked around him at the people he held in high regard, he brought his behavior in line to meet the norms of his new group. He used the social situation, which has been defined by his peers, to determine what's acceptable. Before moving forward, let's briefly explain this thought.

Before Senior Correctional Officer Joseph Hill enters the situation, he may be somewhat unsure of what is truly happening. Therefore, he will look to others within his group for guidance. We can see this happening when he enters the scene and sees the three officers trampling the secured inmate. When he looks to the response team (his peers) to give guidance, or to define the situation, he sees that the team has already entered the situation and decided to join along on the assault on the inmate. Since he stands unsure, he will assume that the group is correct in their actions and follow suit. As mentioned above, this is known as informative influence. Senior Correctional Officer Joseph Hill was unsure of the situation he was facing and went to the group for the information needed. He trusted the information because he trusted the individuals providing it.

Now, by using the information above, let's see if we can find another reason why Senior Correctional Officer Joseph Hill would conform. (Remember, conforming is different than obedience. Conforming is a change in an individual's thought process. Obedience is just following a directive without question. For obedience, an individual follows the directive because they may fear the consequence.) For this perspective, Senior Correctional Officer Joseph Hill knows that what the officers are doing is wrong, but he follows suit anyway. "Why," you may ask. The answer is simple, yet complex. He follows suit because he does not want to be seen as an outcast. As mentioned above, this type of conformity reflects a normative influence. Senior Correctional Officer Joseph Hill conformed to actions that go against his beliefs because he fears the social rejection that would follow if he dissents from the group.

Now, there are other factors at play here that aid in Senior Correctional Officer Joseph Hill's conformity. First, we have group size. Studies have shown that people are more likely to conform if they are in a group with three to five individuals. Now, if Senior Correctional Officer Joseph Hill happened to come across a scene in which it was him and just one other officer and the other officer began to trample the inmate, there is a better chance that Senior Correctional Officer Joseph Hill would not conform to the actions of that one officer. Also, another factor that must be mentioned is group unanimity. In this case, all of Senior Correctional Officer Joseph Hill's peers were involved. Being that they all agreed as determined by their actions, Senior Correctional Officer Joseph Hill would have stood outside the box as an outcast. Had there been just one defector, Senior Correctional Officer Joseph Hill would have unknowingly been influenced by that defector and not conformed.

Moving forward, there is, yet, another factor that can cause conformity: group status. In this case, we know Senior Correctional Officer Joseph Hill admires and trust his peers. It is through that admiration and trust, Senior Correctional Officer Joseph Hill will find himself following them blindly. Also, when there is a trust and admiration for the members of the group you belong to, the group becomes very tight knit. This brings us to our next factor, group cohesiveness. We mentioned this with scenario one and it quickly comes back into play in scenario two. If Senior Correctional Officer Joseph was not connected with the group, he would feel no need to go along with the group. Therefore, the bond that was made in isolation from the other group (inmates) now helps to solidify his connection with his newly formed group (staff). This bond could have been built by discussions between staff members that strengthen the animosity with staff and inmates (group polarization).

We also have observed behavior. If there was someone from the public, not connected to either group, observing the behavior, Senior Correctional Officer Joseph Hill may have found himself less likely to conform. Reason being, if Senior Correctional Officer Joseph Hill believes that, by not conforming, he will be met with public acceptance, he will have the support needed to continue with the behaviors that are aligned with his core beliefs.

Now, Senior Correctional Officer Joseph Hill can conform in one of two ways. He can privately conform and change his behaviors and opinions to align with the group, or he can publicly conform and change superficially (he will outwardly agree with the group, but, on the inside, his beliefs have not changed). Therefore, when he privately conforms to the actions of his peers, he will be convinced that what he did was right, but, when he publicly conforms to an action, he is not sincerely convinced that his actions, and the actions of his peers, was correct.

I want to add another note before closing. If, at any time, before this one incident occurred, Senior Correctional Officer Joseph Hill, had found himself in a situation similar, his actions during the prior situation would determine the likelihood that he would have conformed, or not, in a similar, subsequent, incidences. This would fall under our need to be consistent with who we are. If he had stopped an assault on an inmate in a prior situation, there is a greater likelihood he would have remained consistent with his prior actions and stopped this assault. On the flipside, if he got involved in the beating, or remained motionless in a prior situation, there is a greater chance that he would remain consistent and either got involved in the beating, or froze.

At this point, correctional staff should be familiar with "The Anatomy of a Setup," or "The Downing of a Duck." If they aren't, they can easily Google the two phrases mentioned above and read through the many results that will surface. In short, "The Anatomy of a Setup," or "The Downing of a Duck," refers to a process in which a manipulative inmate progressively gains leverage on the correctional staff member, by using minimal compliance that will later be used to compromise.

Minimal compliance, in this case, refers to the little progressive requests/favors that are granted by staff that seem superficial at first, but, in the long run, will lead to the ultimate request. Due to the leverage that was gained, the inmate will threaten to turn the staff member in if they do not comply with the request given. That, in essence, is a brief description of "The Anatomy of a Setup," or "The Downing of a Duck." But, here is the question, "why does this method work?"

Robert Cialdini Rules of Influence

For this chapter, there will be no opening scenario. Instead, scenarios will be presented next to the rule that is being introduced, so we can see each rule play out in a separate manner. Robert Cialdini conducted a 2 ½ year study on the training programs of the different influence professions. He wanted to understand the tactics that are employed in order to get someone to say "yes." Through this study, Robert Cialdini figured out that there were only 6 universal rules of influence that was being used by these training programs. These 6 rules of influence are **_commitment and consistency_** (the desire to be consistent with what we already said and did/to be congruent with one's internal values), *reciprocity* (the desire to give back to someone who has given to us), *social validity* (the idea that people want to follow the lead of similar others), *authority* (we hold a sense of duty, or obligation, to people in positions of authority), *liking* (we are more likely to be influenced by people we like) and *scarcity* (the desire to have those things you can have less of).

Commitment and Consistency

This one is not so easy to explain, so bear with me. First and foremost, human beings have a need/want to be consistent. Being consistent provides an individual with a sense of comfortability in knowing that their values, attitudes and beliefs are consistent with each other. It also helps them maintain a sense of self control and a view from others that they are reliable. (Now, who doesn't want to have a sense of self control and be seen by others as reliable?) Therefore, once an individual has committed to a behavior, the need to be consistent with that behavior becomes paramount. This need/want for consistency can be easily played upon by the manipulative inmate because consistency is an internal motivation that is not seen on the surface. The manipulative inmate knows this fact. Remember, in regards to "anatomy of a setup," or "the downing of a duck," the manipulative inmate is trying to get the staff member to commit to an initial goal which is consistent with the more important goal the manipulative inmate will request later. The power to be consistent is often invisible, but still has a tremendous affect on who we are. Let's explore this, shall we?

It starts when an inmate walks up to a staff member and makes a simple request. The request is rather small and is only being used as a way to test the staff's member's resolve. The reason why the request starts out small is because the inmate has yet to gain the leverage needed to begin the process of the setup. Also, by starting off small, the staff member may not be that quick to put up their guard. If, without any leverage, the manipulative inmate was to begin with a request for something big and outright noticeable, the staff member would go directly into high alert. So, again, the manipulative inmate is covert with their method by keeping the request small and subtle at first. This is in contrary to what the public may think. The public thinks that the manipulative inmate just makes one big request (drugs, cell phones, etc.) and the correctional staff member is quick to oblige. That is not the case.

Once the staff member crosses the line and gives into the initial request, multiple factors are now in play. First, the inmate now has the leverage needed to move forward. Each progressive step will involve the use of what was granted at the prior step as a threat to get the staff member to comply. This is rather overt and can easily be seen by the staff member once they refuse to comply.

Before we go deeper into consistency, let's talk about another part of the process that is rather covert and can't directly be seen on the surface. This process highlights the use of small and subtle steps. It is the use of these small and subtle steps that makes this process so successful. As the process is played out by the manipulative inmate, the steps are so small and subtle that each request granted by the soon to be compromised staff member is only being compared to the step before. This means, if the first request is granted, the second request doesn't seem so bad by comparison. Moving forward, when the second request gets granted, now, the third request doesn't seem so bad in comparison with the second. The problem here is that instead of the staff member looking at step one upon each request, they look at the step prior. Being that each request is so small and subtle, it becomes hard to find fault in the present request if the request prior was granted. So, in essence, instead of the staff member looking all the way down and seeing how far they have traveled, they look at the current step they are on and compare it with the prior step that they have already taken, and if they find fault with the current step that they are on, then there must have been fault with the step that was just taken moments before.

As the inmate progressively moves up, in accordance with the request that the staff member has granted (minimal compliance), consistency becomes a way for the staff member to protect themselves from admitting they have done anything wrong. If, at any point, they break away from that consistency, the staff member will have to look at their past actions and find fault. This will mean, as they look backwards, that they have the chance of discovering that the line of professionalism has been crossed numerous of times. So, in self defense, they remain consistent in their current behavior in order to rid themselves of wrong doing and fault, which should lie in direct opposition of their beliefs and values.

So now, the staff member is at, what Social Psychologists would call a *cognitive dissonance*. Which simply means, their actions are counter to their beliefs? Therefore, a tension is formed that can only lessen by making their beliefs go in alignment with their actions. So, the compromised staff member will now justify their actions by remaining consistent and defending their position.

Now, what can we do when we see that a staff member may be falling victim to the setup, or might be overly involved with an inmate? This is a tough question to answer. If we accuse the staff member of being to close, they will become defensive, deny wrong doing and remain consistent with what they have been doing. At this point, we must remember, the compromised staff member has found a way to justify their actions to keep their behavior and values in sync. So, this can be a dangerous approach by the concerned staff member because this approach may reinforce the connection between the compromised staff member and the inmate. If the staff member was to listen to their concerned peer and acknowledge what their peer has said, then they will have to admit to themselves that they have done something wrong. This is counter intuitive to their recent justification and they will now have to try to identify when the wrong initially occurred. For them, it is easier to protect themselves from admitting they did wrong (wrong = consequence), as opposed to admitting fault and questioning their many actions that led them to this point.

So, the only thing we can do in this situation is report it. It is better to be wrong and report, then be right and don't. On another note, if, and when, a staff member gets setup and they are finally caught, all their co-workers should be in shock because, if they are not, then they knew something and failed to act.

Reciprocity

Moving forward, we now have reciprocity. Let's start off this section with a quote written by me for an article that was published by corrections.com, *"There are no favors to be granted by an inmate to correctional staff. Favors are considered to be a key tactic used by the inmate population to foster obligation. Obligation is defined as an act or course of action to* which a person is morally or legally bound; a duty or commitment. This definition listed above is the main reason why correctional staff is not in the business of giving and receiving favors. There is no time in our career in which we, as correctional staff, should feel that we are morally or legally bound to actions dictated by the inmate population that lies outside our prescribed roles. Feelings of obligation can lead to favors committed by staff that can jeopardize the safety and integrity of the agency in which we are employed. Obligation to an inmate can blind correctional staff and limit their ability to see the potential threat that a returned favor can produce.

If an inmate comes to your area and volunteers to help you, you need to ask yourself, "why?" What is this inmate expecting in return? If the word favor has been employed, you need to make that inmate aware that we, as correctional staff, are not in the business of giving, or receiving favors. If the inmate is given an order to do something, then it becomes the inmate's responsibility to do it to the best of their means. There will be no sidebar in which the inmate tells staff, "I only go the extra mile for you and if there is anything else you need, don't hesitate to ASK". First off, we, as correctional staff, do not ask. Asking implies that the inmate has a choice to either say "yes" or "no" to your REQUEST. If that is the case, saying "yes" by the inmate can be interpreted as a favor being granted. Correctional staff must be made aware that you are to give your order in a professional manner in which respect is given, but there is no option within your order for a response that lies outside the affirmative. If correctional staff gives an order disguised as a request ("can you...," "if you don't mind....."), then you are giving the inmate the opportunity to change your order into a favor being granted. By this standard, the inmate will be given the chance to employ a sense of obligation that can be used as a way to garner favors for susceptible staff members.

In closing, we are all aware of giving orders in a professional manner. Having said that, these are orders and should never is disguised as a request. Request, in essence, may make the inmate think they have a choice and, if that is the case, your granted request by the inmate population will be seen as a favor that may lead correctional staff into feelings of obligation."

. This article doesn't just talk about the power of obligation; it talks about the power of reciprocity. Reciprocity simply means the need/want to give back. This is a very powerful technique that can easily be employed by the manipulative inmate. This technique, if used properly, can cause a state of tension for the staff member. No one likes to be in debt to someone else. So, when a manipulative inmate tries to employ tactics that begin with key words like "favor," it's a game being played. This tactic being employed is only being used to make the staff member feel obligated. Once the staff member gets that sense of obligation, they will feel the internal need to alleviate that feeling. Therefore, they will feel the need to pay back the debt they think they owe the inmate. But, this is prison, and there are no favors. The job the inmate did was a directive, given by the staff member that requires no payback and no sense of obligation.

SOCIAL VALIDITY

Another tactic that a manipulative inmate likes to employ involves the use of a technique called social validation. A manipulative inmate may come up to Officer with a request. The Officer is unsure about their response to the request and, as mentioned at the beginning of the book, when we are unsure, or in a state of ambiguity, we look to others to define the situation for us. Well, in this case, when the Officer becomes hesitant with their answer, or the "no" seems weak, the manipulative inmate will be quick to state, "We do this all the time when Officer

Smith is here." "Officer Smith" is being used by the inmate as a point of social validity to lift the state of ambiguity and provide the inmate with an affirmative response.

Let's looks at this technique a little closer so we can develop a better understanding of what's at play. Take a second to look at the choice of words the manipulative inmate employs. The word "We" signifies a partnership. At this point, the staff member should ask themselves, "Who is we?" In this case, "we" could mean the inmate population and Officer Smith. "Why Officer Smith," you may ask. That is a great question that has a very definitive answer. The manipulative inmate uses Officer Smith as a reference because Officer Smith is, by being an officer and being put in a position of authority, very similar to the Officer in question. Therefore, when this above mentioned officer is unsure of which action to take (should the officer grant, or refuse, the request), the manipulative inmate is quick to mention someone similar (situational context) that can easily relate to the officer in question. This is an attempt to move any state of ambiguity the officer might have.

By mentioning the officer's peers, the inmate is telling the officer its okay because others in your same situation have done the same. The inmate's choice to use someone the officer can relate to is key for the social validation needed to rid the officer of their sense of ambiguity and doubt. Had the inmate chose to use another inmate, or someone below the officer's level of authority, the plan would not work because these relationships may be seen by the officer as inferior and doesn't contain enough power needed to lift the officer from their state of ambiguity into the affirmative.

In essence, the manipulative inmate makes a borderline request. The officer is in doubt, which can be easily seen. The officer has no place of social reference to help them make a decision. The manipulative inmate is quick to mention that others, who can be seen by the officer as an individual on the same level, have said "yes" in the past. This is a tactic by the inmate to remove any sense of doubt. Social validation has now been created by the manipulative inmate. The officer takes what the inmate says at face value and, therefore, agrees to the request. Inmate gets what they want. Inmate walks away knowing they change the officer's mind simply by alleviating the officer's doubt. How, you may ask? The inmate was quick to respond to the officer's sense of doubt by using someone the officer can relate to and having that someone become the social validation needed for the request to be granted.

Authority

Authority is defined as "power over another." In the prison system, inmates are looking for ways to circumvent authority. The manipulative inmate is looking to attain power over staff and gain a sense of control within in the system. At this point, we already should be aware of overt methods of leverage that is used to maintain authority and force compliance ("Downing a Duck"), but what about the covert?

In regards to authority, inmates will do whatever they can to gain a sense of control. Some methods can be seen and others can be felt, but both, if successful, can be very dangerous. A covert method that manipulative inmates like to employ is based on associations. In essence, those individuals who are closest to those in power can sometimes be seen in the same light. Let's be honest, as a baseline staff member, we may find ourselves feeling inferior when talking to the Warden's secretary. We may feel that way because of their immediate connection, or association, with the higher level staff member. Through their connection, or association, they are seen at the same level and, therefore, we may unknowingly put ourselves at a lower level.

A manipulative inmate is very much aware of the power of *association*. They are aware that, if a connection is made between them and a higher level staff member, baseline staff members may see the inmate in the same light as they see their bosses. The manipulative inmate will be quick to let staff know that the connection exist and will have no problem dropping the name of a higher up when they are either looking to get their way, or avoid trouble. The manipulative inmate wants this connection to be visible and wants those on the lower end to see it. Once it becomes known, and the inmate is seen by staff as being connected with the higher level, the inmate's ability to gain a sense of authority is slowly beginning to come to fruition.

With that connection, or association, in play, a baseline staff member may feel either less enthused to do their job, or less able. They may even find themselves defending the inmate, so they can gain favor with the higher up. It's sad to say, but in some cases, the inmate may even have a better chance of seeing and conversing with a higher level staff member than baseline staff. So, in an effort for baseline staff to attain the higher up's approval, the inmate is now seen as a go between.

This is why it is paramount for higher level staff members to always remember to be professional with inmates. If you make it known that you show favor to the inmate population, by associating yourself with the inmate population, your power of authority is slowly being given to the inmates in question. The staff members on the lower end will see that connection and, through that connection, some will become hesitant to do their job. Remember, manipulative inmates are out to exploit any connection, or association, they can gain with staff and they will keep that relationship going as long as they receive favor. That little conversation about sports with that inmate in the day room, in front of everyone, is only a tactic. It is simply meant to make the connection with higher level staff visible and make those on the lower end feel inferior. If that connection continues to pursue, through association with higher level staff members, the manipulative inmate will gain the authority needed to say "no" and not be charged. Associate with your support staff and let the inmates know that your bond with your support staff can never be broken.

Friendliness/Likability

Let's admit one thing; it is harder to tell people that we like, "no." A manipulative inmate wants the staff member to like them. They want the staff member to connect with them on a level that goes beyond professionalism. In their eyes, they want the staff member to see them, not as an inmate, but as a human being with similar needs, likes and interests. They want to connect and that connection is meant to exploit the staff member and help the inmate reach their wanted objective.

First and foremost, when a manipulative inmate finds out personal information about a staff member, they have just received an open door to attain a personal connection. The manipulative inmate wants the staff member to forget they are an inmate. If the staff member forgets that they are dealing with an inmate, they begin to forget their prescribed roles they are trusted to perform. In order for an inmate to accomplish this goal, the inmate will try to identify with the staff member on a personal level. For example, if the staff member talks about their children a lot, the manipulative inmate will get a sense of how important family is to this staff member. Now, in order for the inmate to foster a connection, they may fabricate how important their kids are to them and use that as a way to connect with the staff member. Eventually, conversations pursue and that connection is made. Now, the staff member no longer sees the inmate as an inmate, but rather someone with the same needs and interest as them. Now, the role of inmate has been removed and in its place is a title that connects the inmate to staff on a personal level (parent, sibling, race, religion, etc). This can make the staff member become sympathetic to the inmate's needs/wants because the staff member begins to see similarities based on the stories that are being employed by the manipulative inmate. Once sympathy has formed, the staff member becomes blinded by emotion and can no longer be effective in the prescribed role. It essence, it becomes harder for the staff member to tell the inmate "no."

As a side bar, below is a quick article I wrote for corrections.com that explains the differences with empathy and sympathy. It is okay to be empathetic, but, by no means, are we to be sympathetic.

Sympathy vs. Empathy

You will find that there have been recent discussions taking place on multiple forums in regards to empathy making individuals vulnerable. Empathy is defined as the ability to share and understand the feelings of others. By this definition, being empathetic is considered objective because a true understanding of the feelings of others cannot be blinded by emotion. In the correctional setting, staff may confuse empathy with sympathy. Sympathy is defined as a mutual affinity towards another and, by definition, sympathy can lead to pity. By this standard, sympathy can be seen as more subjective and, therefore, may lead an individual down a path where they become emotionally blinded.

Being empathetic is by no means exposing vulnerability. On the contrary, empathy can be a powerful tool. It relates us to the situation, or individual, in an objective manner that helps aid in the choices that we make. You are able to relate to the experience at hand in a way that promotes understanding, but not pity. In essence, I understand how it is to be in your shoes and, therefore, there is no need for me to wear them. Inmates will do what they can to promote a relationship that centers on a proposed similarity between them and staff that creates a mutual affinity (sympathy). This tactic used by inmates is meant to blind us from seeing them as an inmate. This tactic exploits a chance by the inmate to remove the title of inmate and connect on a level that relates to the shared experience that they are trying to create with staff (father/son/etc). At this level, personal information that has been gathered by the inmate furthers their chances of success in regards to building a rapport that lies outside of the staff member's defined boundaries. The staff member, relating to the inmate's story, which has been manufactured and centered around their personal life of the staff member, may begin to feel the emotional tug that will eventually form sympathy. In essence, sympathy is built on the shared experience that has been manufactured in an attempt to emotionally blind the staff member. In this case, sympathy has been built through the personal experience of the staff member and now the inmate will exploit their connection to the staff by pushing forward their proposed shared experience that highlights a fictional bond.

The situation now becomes dangerous for the staff member because the title of inmate, as viewed by the staff member, has been removed and in its place becomes the connection needed for the inmate to move forward with their plan. At this point, the inmate has taken the staff member's story, their personal life, and built a scenario that persuades the staff member to stand outside their uniform and see the inmate in a manner that connects him or her to themselves on a personal level. The staff member may find themselves feeling sorry for the inmate because the false bond that has been built is created by using the vulnerability of the staff member. In essence, the staff member cannot help but see themselves in the inmate because the story the *inmate has created is based on the life of the staff member. The staff member has now become blinded by emotion and may feel the need to help this inmate rise above their dilemma.*

As for empathy, empathy is an understanding of the situation at hand, but remaining objective. Even if the inmate tries to use obtained personal information about staff, the staff member may be able to relate to the story, but it will not, in any manner, have an effect on how the staff member does their job. Empathy, in other words, provides staff with the ability to see how it is to be in the inmate's shoes without having to walk in them. By this standard, the staff member will not be blinded by the emotions that come with sharing a troubled journey. The staff member is able to separate their problems from their profession and, therefore, they have a sense of control that will not blind them emotionally to the inmate.

In some cases, arguments will pursue in regards to empathy and sympathy making staff vulnerable. From my perspective I have to seriously disagree. Sympathy is subjective. In our profession, sympathy can relate to the inability to separate yourself emotionally from the problems of another. Sympathy brings pity and blinds you from seeing the situation in a truly objective manner. Empathy, in essence, is objective. Empathy is the understanding of situation in a manner that is not blinded by emotion. Empathy helps us see how it is to walk in someone else's shoes without the need to wear them. It creates the boundary that is needed to understand the situation, but still remain separate from it. In my eyes, empathy builds understanding in a manner that helps us adapt. Empathy is not, nor ever will be, an emotional connection forcing us blindly to the choices we will later regret. Empathy is a tool that builds rapports and maintains the level of professionalism needed to work in an environment in which new situations arise and our safety depends on how we react.

Scarcity

The final rule, Scarcity, is a tactic that can easily be employed to a desperate staff member. If the inmate discovers that the staff member is in dire need of something, they may quickly step up and be the hero. For example, a staff member finds himself to be in a financial strain. He is broke and bills are due. Rumors have spread through the prison that his house is ready to be taken back by the bank. Well here comes inmate Peter Williams. Inmate Peter Williams has a solution for this staff member's problems. Inmate Peter Williams tells the troubled staff member that he can pay him a substantial fee if he is willing to bring contraband into the facility. He then tells the staff member that he has to act quickly or else the offer will be gone. The officer in desperation quickly agrees to the inmates requests.

Even though this may sound rather idiotic by the staff member, he was in a desperate situation and became vulnerable to the solution the inmate had to offer. That is why it is important to not make it known that a fellow staff member is in a dire situation. If a manipulative inmates gets wind that the staff member may be desperate, the inmate will have the quick solution that will eventually compromise the safety and security of the prison, or jail in which the compromised staff member is employed.

If anything…remember this….

Remember, an inmate will look for anyway to connect with staff. That connection is meant to be personal and bring a staff member out of their defined role as a professional employee. When dealing with inmates, staff members must remember the role they play, the job they are being trusted to perform, and the immediate group in which the staff member belongs. In short, an inmate will look to connect with staff based on the staff member's personal similarities and interests. Once that connection is made, staff will be pulled from the role they play and placed in a role that is outside of their prescribed duties. Now, the inmate has a chance to connect with the staff member on that outside role by pulling the staff member into a group that relates to this fabricated personal connection (parent, race, religion, etc). Now, the staff perception of the inmate has been altered. The inmate is no longer an inmate, they are a parent, a sibling etc. With that connection made and the relationship that is now built, the human element takes over and sympathy will follow. If, and when, sympathy surfaces, that staff member will now become emotionally blinded to the needs and wants of the manipulative inmate. Remember, never forget the role you are being trusted to perform and, remember, anything outside that role will lead you to being compromised.

Below, you will find some articles that I have written that have been published either through correctionsone.com, or corrections.com. Enjoy.

Abuse of Authority and Why We Fail to React

We have seen time and time again, the abuse of authority and the failure from others to intervene. Countless videos have been documented in which a correctional officer can be seen as being aggressive towards an inmate, while there are other officers, that are present, who fail to act accordingly. We quickly begin to think that "if we were in the same predicament, we would have done the right thing and stopped the officer from abusing their sense of authority." But, we need to ask ourselves, is it really that simple?

When we look at the videos and see the individuals abusing their sense of authority, we are seeing the video from a different perspective than seen from those, who at that time, went through it. From our perspective, we already know what has happened and, therefore, the actions that were required. In short, this scene has been defined already and we are using that definition to guide us in our reflective response.

Now, for those who lived it, they are seeing this happen live and, therefore, they are in search of a way to define this novel situation. When they look towards others to define the situation and they see that no one is making an attempt to stop this abuse of authority, the person looking to define the situation may begin to use those who remain motionless as a key part in that definition. They may wrongly assume that those who have failed to act have failed to act because they believe that the need to act is unnecessary, unwise, or inappropriate.

On another note, since there are multiple bystanders present, we now have diffusion of responsibility at play. With more than one person being held responsible, if the individual is wrong and there was a need to react, the guilt for not acting can be spread out.

This brings us to another point, if there was only one person seeing the abuse occur, would there be a greater chance they would intervene? The answer is yes. First, if they are the only one witnessing the act, they cannot look to others to define the situation for them. As mentioned above, when there are multiple bystanders, the failure to act by others can be seen by the individual as unnecessary, unwise, or inappropriate. But, when they are by themselves, there is no one to give that meaning. So, they have to look inwards. Therefore, when they see a situation where they may believe that authority is being abused, they will lift their sense of ambiguity by reacting.

Also, on another note, if they are by themselves, failure to act in accordance only leaves one person to blame.

In closing, we look to others to define our situation. When we see a video in which there are many witnesses to an act in which no one intervened, we must put ourselves in their shoes. Sometimes the individuals in question wanted to act, but was unsure of what it was they were seeing. Remember, *what seems obvious to us, is only obvious because we know the answer already. For them, the individual living it, the situation is novel and the environment becomes their means to define what they should do next.*

THE MEDIA GETS ITS WRONG!

There are those that are quick to judge what we do from a distance. Their judgment is centered on a belief that is far removed from the stone walls in which we, as correctional officers, patrol. Their belief stems from a world that has been shaped solely for entertainment purposes and, with that in mind, reality has been separated. With entertainment as the only defining perspective of those who are far removed from the authenticity of what we do and what we accomplish, their point of view becomes tainted by both situational and behavioral extremes that are fashioned for no other purpose, but to receive higher ratings.

We can't place fault in the individuals who have received their train of thought from the media, because, being in isolation from what we do, their thirst for knowledge of the unknown will accept all incoming information at face value. Their need for proper validation is limited because the work of corrections is concealed in the shadows of justice and their pursuit for the truth can only be attained from one source, the media.

Again, we cannot fault these individuals because their thirst for knowledge has led them to the only fountain willing to provide them with a drink. Social events, provided by us, in which we, as correctional officers, can attend and spread the word, has been severely limited because our presence is few and far between. We vent, in frustration, for equality with others who enforce the law, but that voice is only at a whisper. In separation, we voice our concerns to a limited few, who remain within our circle, but make no effort to venture out. Our ability to fight, stand tall, and, most importantly, be heard, in regards to who we are and what we represent, remains within the confines of a very small community who has yet to break free from the boundaries of the wall in which they reside.

WHERE IS OUR VOICE? THE TRUE VOICE OF CORRECTIONS! The media has led the way uncontested by those who "walk the walk." They have been the voice of reason to those who seek a better understanding of the elements that make up the correctional system. Unchallenged, the media is able to invent a twisted perspective that the uninformed will blindly follow. We, collectively, need to untwist this perspective and bring to the light the professional work we accomplish deep in the shadows. THIS IS NOT AN OPTION! We are at the point where we need to move forward and be recognized as law enforcement professionals. In order for this above recognition to occur, we cannot stand in isolation from the public. We need to stand united with the public and, during their thirst for knowledge; we need to be the ones that provide them with a drink.

Collectively, we need to stand tall with our brothers and sisters of corrections and, during social events, we need to inform the public that we are law enforcement and our duties are defined by the legal code of the state in which we are employed. Behind the wall, in which we patrol, and away from the public's view, is a society that is built on aggression and predation. Behind the wall is a world filled with individuals looking to usurp the legal powers within and create a utopia that remains lawless and uncontrolled.

Therefore, we, the correctional officers, become the only line of defense between chaos and disorder. In this battle, many have been sacrificed, but only a small few get recognition. There have even been debates about the eternal placement of our fallen and whether they have earned the right, among others in the law enforcement profession, to be remembered in a manner that brings permanent recognition to the civil service they provided. These are senseless debates that can only strive in our silence. If we remain silent and continue our existence in seclusion, the sacrifices that are made by those within the wall will continually fail to reach the level of recognition it has rightfully earned.

WE can no longer stand idle and witness our profession be bastardized by those who have never set foot inside the wall. WE need to speak up and be the voice of reason when the media chooses to belittle our profession. WE need to be proud of the position we have attained and the duties in which we perform. WE need to let the public know that we are the law behind the wall and those that are confined within are kept secured by our sworn duty to protect and serve the public. WE are the ones that hold the keys to fear and civil unrest. WE complete the circle of law enforcement and enforce the rules within so the public can sleep safe at night. If there is any question in regards to who we are and what we stand for, WE NEED TO BE THERE

TO ANSWER SAID QUESTIONS. IN CLOSING, WE NEED TO STAND UNITED AND HAVE OUR VOICES HEARD. WE NEED TO REMOVE OURSELVES FROM THE DARK AND BRING TO LIGHT THE TRUE ROLE OF A CORRECTIONAL OFFICER AND HOW WE WALK THE FINAL LINE BETWEEN CONTROL AND ANARCHY. WE COMPLETE THE CRICLE OF JUSTICE AND STAND UNITED WITH OTHER LAW ENFORCEMENT AGENCIES IN THEIR PURSUIT TO CREATE A SOCIETY THAT CAN PEACEFULLY SLEEP AT NIGHT KNOWING THEIR GREATEST FEARS ARE LOCKED AWAY!

Hearing the Voice from the Frontline: Experience and Education

You are sitting at your desk, waiting for the next inmate movement to be called out over the intercom, when you get approached by your supervisor, who delivers yet, another memo and, just when you are about to ask a question, the supervisor is gone. In frustration, you look over the memo and learn that upper management has implemented a change that, in your experienced opinion, conflicts with the overall performance of your job. You want to say something, but you remain silent. You shake your head in aggravation, recalling how numerous times before your opinion at the bottom level got lost as it began to travel further up the chain of command. .

Disappointed, you again realize that today, like every other day, your voice will not be heard –- that your existence in the system is nothing more than a formality of merely being "just another front line employee," who's professional experience and expertise, as seen from above, has no value.

On a national law enforcement level, experienced officers are being marginalized, in terms of promotions, by those who have attained higher levels of education. Those with college degrees are securing the higher positions and making decisions that can only be made, or understood, by walking the front line.

Let's be honest, in today's world, the collective voice of just professional experience, especially from the front line, will lose its volume as it travels up. What you may hear as a scream at the bottom level becomes, but, a whisper as it moves upwards, muted by the many obstacles along the way.

On a side note, even if by chance, the proverbial whisper is heard by the "powers that be," it's is sometimes perceived by upper management as a personal attack. So, again, in fear of a potential conflict, you hold back your experienced opinion and harbor whatever thoughts you have and deal with the shortsighted changes that will occur.

Your failure to speak and their unwillingness to listen becomes the repeated cycle that will eventually define your career. Through this repetition, the morale of those on the front line lessens as they become mere automatons going through the motions that were delegated from those who choose to lead in a manner where communication simply moves only in a downward flow. Eventually, this form of leadership is begrudgingly accepted and those with professional experience remain in the dark.

As is all paramilitary structures, you cannot go against directives. As you already know, you must remain subordinate to the system, but that does not mean that you are out of options. There is a way to level the promotional playing field and, therefore, secure the positions of leadership that will promote the changes needed by those on the front line.

Now, in order for you to begin your move upwards, you must first educate yourself! This is paramount. You need to earn the degrees necessary that will help you secure the higher leadership positions and bring experience back to the upper echelons of command.

But make sure, once you begin your journey upwards and secure those positions, that you remember where you came from and maintain open communication with those who still walk the front line. Too often, those who get promoted "fail to remember" the needs and perspectives of those who still reside on the lower level of command.

Don't be like the many officers who silently vent their frustration to others and never move beyond the grumbling. Be the elite, who move beyond the grumbling and vow that collectively, "the voices of the frontline will be heard." In the shadows, they seek and attain the education needed to bring the voices of the front line to the upper managerial positions. They remain true to their roots and bring back the level of experience needed to reflect the immediate needs of the front line staff.

Brothers and Sisters, if one's true motivation to move upwards is powered by the voices of the front line, then they are making a selfless sacrifice in an effort to maintain the balance needed to compliment experience with education..

We all know corrections have evolved and there is a need for those with degrees in psychology, sociology, and business administration. We know to look at the whole picture and see things objectively from a standpoint that highlights the multiple departments (mental health, education, social services, religion, etc) and the goals these departments must achieve. With that in mind, safety and security must never be sacrificed in order to obtain the goals of rehabilitation. An officer who has worked with those on the front line will know what decisions to make when an emergency arises and safety and security must be maintained.

But, as of now we must ask ourselves: "Are those with experience being ignored?" Can those who are involved in making the final decision during an emergency safely say that the degree that they have earned has given them the experience needed to lead matters in an efficient and safe manner? In all honesty, education alone cannot replace experience.

Therefore, it is my personal opinion that officers with professional experience should not just compliment, but supersede those with degrees. Those, at the front line, who have defined their careers by remaining professional and true to the badge they have sworn to uphold, are looking to be recognized and appreciated. As experience continues to get overlooked, custodial staff needs to take the road less traveled and secure the positions that will give birth to the many voices from within. But in order to do so, higher education may be the only option you have to level the promotional playing field.

The Importance of Cross-Gender Supervision

There are obvious arguments against cross-gender supervision that remain rather primitive and deal directly with older methods of jailing with no regards for rehabilitation. These older methods relate to the old-fashion turnkey style of lock up, where no effort is made to prevent recidivism and interactions with the inmate population was extremely limited. Being that corrections have evolved and more effort is now being geared towards rehabilitation, correctional officers are now being force to interact with the inmate population in a more productive and detailed manner.

   If corrections were kept in the shadows, with no attempt to evolve, then cross-gender supervision would be obsolete. There would be no need for balance because there would be no effort from the higher ups to create a world, within a world, where rehabilitation superseded punishment. To the uninformed, those who remain on the outside, this is the world that exist. In their minds, inmates stay confined within their cells until their final day of imprisonment has been reached. During their stay, inmates remain in solitude and interactions with staff occur at a bare minimum. Again, this is the world that has been created in the minds of the uninformed, which, by this standard, does not reflect reality.

Moving forward, as those in corrections already know, this above mentioned belief is definitely not the case. Inmate movements occur throughout the day. Rehabilitation has defined the inmate's way of life while incarcerated and, throughout the day, a constant effort must be maintained by correctional staff so the inmate can leave the facility in a manner that is stable and conducive to society's norms. By this standard, cross-gender supervision provides the inmate with a true sense of reality.

By limiting the inmate to same-gender supervision, their ability to interact properly with the opposite gender will become strictly limited to past practices. In some cases, these past practices are deeply rooted by the negative interactions with the opposite gender that have scarred the individual in the first place.

If we are looking to send forth an adjusted individual, we can not underestimate the power behind cross-gender supervision. If we look to rehabilitate, we need to create, as much as possible, a true reflection of the outside world. Failure to create that sense of realism will severely limit any attempt to rehabilitate.

Recent attempts by Federal standards are being made to prevent interactions between officers of opposite gender and the inmates that reside within their line of authority. These recent attempts have generalized all officers of opposite-gender as one bad seed that must be eliminated. This generalization is unfair because it creates a stigma without any sense of regard towards those who, even though they are opposite of gender, remain professional in their duties and have proven themselves to be an asset on all needed levels of the agency. Generalization, like the one mentioned above, become the centerpiece in which the uninformed derive their legislation. This generalization presents a sense of dishonor to those who have held themselves true to the badge they are sworn to uphold. Eventually, through unfair legislation, certain officers will be looked at as a liability, as opposed to being seen as true professionals.

In closing, I would like to highlight one example that can be used as a point of reference. Within this one example, an honest debate can manifest, but, keep in mind, that the need to run a safe and secure facility is still paramount. But, since we have evolved, we must make room for secondary necessities, like rehabilitation, that can be maintained only through an orderly and secured facility. It is through these secondary necessities that true adjustment by the inmate will occur. Having said that, any attempt for a successful adjustment made by the inmate can only occur if the inmate is exposed to real life situations that will continue to challenge their negative view of the opposite-gender.

My example relates to a female who was constantly abused by male aggressors. This abuse caused her to react in a manner that led to her incarceration. During incarceration, her time is now spent away from the opposite-gender. At this point, she begins to further develop her sense of fear and disgust towards males. This sense of fear and disgust now becomes deeply embedded in who she is because, within that sense of fear and disgust, she has learned to justify her crime. Therefore, to keep that state of mind balanced, she may generalize the action of just the few to the many. Now, being in continued isolation from the opposite-gender, her pervasive perspective becomes her foundation of belief towards her gender counterpart. She cannot see outside the box because she is limited to what's inside her head. Her limited dealings with the opposite-gender will not break her away from the corrupted thoughts that have now become the backbone of her existence while in isolation.

Being that corrections now looks to rehabilitate, cross-gender supervision will create the dissonance needed to challenge her pervasive perspective and create the alternative perspective needed, which will highlight the proper role model for outside adjustment. In essence, the need for cross-gender supervision runs parallel with rehabilitation. If we stand and limit the need for cross-gender interaction and supervision, the inmate will remain with the original frame of reference which will follow them upon release and then bring them right back in prison.